Song of the Middle Manager

Song of the Middle Manager

Poems
Richard Cole

GRAYSON BOOKS
West Hartford, Connecticut
graysonbooks.com

Song of the Middle Manager is a book about work and the human spirit, about the sacrifice and gain we can find in the business world, our daily lives, and the labor of creation.

Acknowledgments

Some poems from *Song of the Middle Manager* have appeared in the following publications:

Barrow Street: The Man Who Was Passed Over; Song of the Middle Manager

Cloudbank: Opening Windows

Dappled Things: This Trip; Learning to Paint

Diode: Working for the Pyramid; Mergers & Acquisitions

Image Journal: ICU, Four a.m.; Walking in Circles

MacQueen Quinterly: Understanding Markets

Main Street Rag: Oh Dear

Prairie Schooner: St. Francis in Prayer; Ashes; To Get to the Other Side

Presence: Manifest Destiny

Rattle: How Much Does Your House Weigh?

Ruminate: The Beauty of a Strip Mall; Rothko's Chapel

Sixfold: Triage; Perfect Corporations; Too Big to Fail; Becoming Air

Texas Observer: The House That Brochures Built

THAT Literary Review: Admission; Home Depot

The American Journal of Poetry: Chapter Eleven; Initial Public Offering

The Penn Review: After the Accident

The Woven Tale Press: Being of Two Minds; Outsider Art

Waxwing: Deepwater Horizon

Windhover: The Silence of God

Contents

Best Practices

Mortal Business

The Beauty of a Strip Mall

is the beauty of a minor
dream turned quietly
aside at the end of the day,
the beauty of the small,
impossible ledgers recording
hope against subtraction and finally
closed with a sigh.

Every unremarkable donut shop
is somebody's act of faith,
and somewhere between almost and
never quite, in the last miles
of aging neon and plastic
backlit signage, here
too is poetry, where the books
will someday be balanced and the future
is always a bargain, everything
ninety-nine cents.

The House That Brochures Built

My finest work, to be honest —
the thousands of slick,
four-color brochures to support
my wife, myself, two sons and a home,
selling life insurance and security
bonds, selling porta-toilets
and hard cheese, selling faith,
reassurance and calm.

I've lit candles for clients
and prayed for their welfare
and prayed for their business,
and for years I've prayed for the copy
and the copy has come, well-
hacked and sweated, typing the words
that work for these artful books,
songs of myself, each one
my best shot,
none of them signed.

This Trip

Third day of the hurricane
and the whole world is flooded,
neighbors huddled on rooftops,
and that's when the father and son
arrive, in an outboard,
and the people clamber down,
stiff-legged, shivering, and with so many souls
loading the boat that the son says
I'll get out, and he trades places
with the last ones so all are saved
this trip. The father nods,
makes a promise and heads upriver,
leaving his son behind,
surrounded by rising water,
waiting in the steady rain
for the empty boat to return.

Song of the Middle Manager

I have walked down silent corporate hallways
deep in the belly. I have worn the white shirts of fire
with muted tie, dark shoes and matching wallet.

I have eaten the cocktail wienie
at company picnics and listened to the bosses
and admired their muscular toys.

I have laughed with the eager lieutenants.
I have kissed ass and pondered.

I have watched over my unwavering people
and watched them disappear into void.
I have cleaned out my desk.
I have felt a company go under.

I have passed through the walls of yellow smoke
and emerged, squinting, on the other side
and consulted with the prophets of caffeine
charting apocalypse — who will be saved
and who will be marked as losers.

I have lost my dreams
in exchange for others smaller and stronger.

I have caught the last flight out of Omaha.
I have made my connections.

And at times, alone in the early morning,
somewhere between the parking lot
and divided office, between the checks
and daily inches of accommodation,
I have seen such beauty in the air
and paused, if only for a moment.

I have gone so far and not gone further.
I have walked through other doorways filled with light.

To Get to the Other Side

After Kay Ryan

We think it's a joke,
and so we are, here
in the rain, in our yellow
slickers and chicken feet
beside the road,
waiting for the obvious
punch line once it's
punched and crossing
forever as long
as we cross for the mother
of all proud reasons —
to get to the other
because it's
there, not here
where others are.

Working for the Pyramid

Whipped like rocks, we're all Egyptians
working for death, for the pure idea
of capital numbers, tonnage
tricked and heaved up muddy slopes,
our own bodies the engines of increase,
spirit-shells boxed shoulder to shoulder and leashed
to a dream of freedom greater than labor,
labor stronger than pride.

With pride, then, we assume the soft
ropes of subordination securing our lives.
We believe in a pyramid, in ordered truth,
in an elevation of command more faithful
than all our cults and mild ambitions.

Stamped and soothed at night with exhaustion,
we lie awake in the cool desert winds,
dreaming of a monument finished,
radiant in all its massiveness,
with distant lights wavering at the top
where unseen leaders travel through the dark
like beautiful insects, shaping the future,
and over us all, the logical moon,
constant and airless, where lesser souls,
becoming shadows on earth, will someday shine.

Mergers & Acquisitions

Flying to the promised land, I dream
of ancient Egyptians, their hollowness,
dead men walking through airports, smiling, extending
their soft hands in recognition…

I lay out my business suit for the trip,
rehearsing my speech, and the beautiful numbers
pour out of me like water.

I believe in our corporation, in the natural
marriage of business and death,
our storm gods and executive furies
striding through terminals,
self-made and acquiring masters
flanked by falcons and honor guards,
low enemies scattering before us like roaches.

We have seen that bewildered look
in the eyes of the dull, tremendous giants
we overtake, so we lay them down
gently on the conference table, opening
their slack and bullish remains
with caution, working through layers
of pure contagion, rot and pockets of fat.
The body jerks and relaxes, bones
melting into silver.

The watchdogs with their manifestos
wish us in hell, stuffed
screaming into burning pipes,
but the soul endures —
spook and little shaving
inch-worming its way to heaven.

So let this other Egypt stand for a world
and let that world be stark and beautiful
like an empty airport at midnight
as I touch down from another country,
my right hand extended, my wings
darkened from flight.

Initial Public Offering

Monitors at dawn. In our cubicles, we stare at the estimated earnings. An hour ahead, the New York market is preparing to open, and we all lean forward. This is our baby offering. Dear God, make it happen. The ticker starts crawling across the bottom of the screen. Our stock opens and the price declines, unsteady. Then it gains 2 dollars.

The floor trembles.

For a moment, the market ponders, watching itself. The stock ticks, ticks, ticks, then ticks up 5 dollars…8…then 12 and surging now, building traction and we take a breath and everyone is suddenly talking…

and like a miracle, on the roof of our office building,
bright sails flair open and belly tight in the wind,
and our building lurches. We feel it start to move,
grinding forward with every window shaking,
market numbers climbing, and we're cheering now,
and the building gathers speed, scraping
over the lawns of the office park, leaving a trail
of raw earth and tiny figures in the parking lot,
and our building severs the freeway,
cars screeching, slamming into each other
as we pass like a grand hallucination, like a dinosaur
crushing the bridges, red lights flashing,
dragging power lines behind us, sparking like wild nerves,
and then suddenly, it's silent. We're in the air. We're flying.

The CEO clears his throat. His eyes glitter
kindly as he stirs his coffee and gets up to speak.
"A billion per year," he says.

A hush fills the room. Our eyes shine like his,
our minds racing as we calculate our options,
and he talks and talks us higher, our knight of faith,
dreamweaver, and the stock keeps gaining confidence,

and we're sailing faster, staring in wonder
as we fly toward a wall of clouds, beautiful clouds,
massive and brilliant, like solid rock.

Dancing in a Business Suit

Which is not about dancing, of course, or business
or dutiful suits but the natural heart,
incarnate and cloistered, still beating its music
through layers of gray, its wiggle and stomp
keeping cold celebration with profits
from driving decisions I heartlessly make
in the dark, as I must, for the bodies I feed.
The heart! The heart! The red-flashing heart!
The palpable business of meat that enriches
the soul intertwined in the thin suits providing
both armor and insight required by the world
where I mortally will not and cannot stop dancing.

The Man Who Was Passed Over

He eats his thrifty
sandwich at noon
with the door closed
halfway, the little bread
cut neatly by his wife, two
pickles, a bag
of delicious chips.

Down the hall, senior
management laughs
at an old joke they tell
on themselves, that war story
about big Jolly puffing
to catch a plane.

"Come in," he says politely,
and offers you a leather
chair with only
the mildest of irony
deep in his eyes, an anger
he saves for himself
at home.

Oh Dear

I take the automatic from the filing cabinet
and head to the corner office where I catch
the Vice President of Software Sales
and he looks up, smiling, his eyes like two
knife slits. "Is this a good time?" I ask
and push three bullets into his chest. Oh
dear. What have I done? The CFO
rushes in. I can't speak for a moment,
overwhelmed. He gets paper towels.
This is our busy season, so the interns
drag the body into the break room
temporarily where people step
around it to get their favorite beverage.
Later, his wife and bewildered children arrive.
She signs the release, and I want to tell her
we all have our deadlines, but she shoots me
a look of white hatred as she walks out the door.
Things calm down eventually, and we hoist
the body to a steel platform on the roof, and his flesh
returns to the sky. We collect the long
bones and bury them under the ficus trees
in reception. We have the skin tanned
and cut into wallets. He was a big man. Many, many wallets,
with the company name stamped in gold on the inside
flap. His skull we keep in the lobby.
We make it our logo, a sign you can trust,
and our company not only survives
but thrives, an industry leader where teamwork
is more than a motto, and success is always
greater than any one person.

Chapter Eleven

We've been up in the air for a while now, the great white sails on the roof holding steady as we bang out the code, each line executable. And even when the revenues faltered, when the market went sideways for six months, then a year, when the last round of funding was abruptly pushed back, then again with deferrals and murmurs, with broad promises and further studies, even then we still had faith.

But the building is losing altitude, and we're starting to hemorrhage, losing cash, and streams of smoke begin trailing furiously past our windows. The gauges are spinning, and doors start slamming as the senior managers walk out of a meeting smiling calmly, hiding the terror behind their eyes, trying to convince us that something is an issue instead of a problem.

Then a jolt. We all feel it.

Then a long shudder and a string of muffled explosions, and the computer screens flicker, almost collapsing in on themselves as the lights dim, recover, then flicker again. And suddenly the company is seized with a new awareness. We're in deep shit and we know it. The copy machines start thumping like combines, spewing out projects, and management scrambles in a frenzy, trimming the fat, throwing out bodies, beating the drums, and the VPs slam down their phones and roar to themselves in silence. We're calling New York, L.A. and Boston. We're calling Cincinnati and the windows are trembling.

Our backer backs away, leaving voice mails and a dry kiss on our foreheads. Hopelessness sweeps the company, accountants staring at their monitors, pupils dilated, searching for answers, and the sales reps chatter brightly on the telephones, "Busy! We're busy! Quite busy!" and the hills are rushing straight toward us and filling the windows and now everyone is screaming.

The building whips across the top of the forest, branches exploding in front of us, and we hit the first hilltop, hard, then a long, terrible second of floating, then another impact, another and we're crashing down into cedar trees and brush, bouncing heavily, bulldozing the rocks in front of us, the building breaking open like an egg, walls collapsing, smoke gushing through the hallways. Then silence.

Whispers across the rubble. The phones are dead. Gradually we pick ourselves up, trying to understand, thinking of next steps and that's when we see them — the strangers approaching through the trees, tall and hooded. Their faces are pale, alien-looking. They fiddle at their calculators with bony fingers, restructuring debt. They compare their numbers. They seem to reach a decision. Without saying a word, they start to lead us, one by one, through the broken trees, along the dirt paths, and we approach the top of the highest cliff. We stop at the edge, and they silently encourage us forward. We hesitate, but they look so intently in our wild, bewildered faces, as if we could teach them, as if we could fly.

Too Big to Fail

The sky is filled with brokers jumping from windows,
some holding hands as they step off together,
showers of suits and ties that flutter
down through crashing markets, debt bombs
going off inside the bundled securities wrapped
and bleeding through layers of gauze,
20 years of financial assumptions collapsing
like circus tents on fire, elephants screaming, old lions
roaring in outrage as the furious band plays on,
and the bodies keep falling faster,
racing to a final moment, the slap
and explosion of meat
hitting the sidewalks, and then
they touch down
gently, as if
on a well of bubbling energy.

"You're safe," the dancing master says.
"You'll always be safe. It's like a love affair
with gravity. Look at what you've already become
and what that means. You've made a killing.
The banks are immortal, in their way,
and so, in a way, are you."

Perfect Corporations

Corporations are people, too,
numbers with skin.

Like people, they have dreams.
Like people, they can ache and grow
and have that growth cut short,
wounded, and then survive
to consume or be consumed by others.
Like people at times, they have
no choice, and the better ones have come to believe
that people, natural people, are frictions,
that the best corporations are heaven on earth
as the earth drops away, trailing numbers,
human capital liquefied
and refined, the corporate body
reorganized by cold explosions leaving
a cloudy taste
and empty cubicles filled with light.

The perfect corporations are the ones
with nobody left, beautifully efficient. The ones
that have no soul.

Economies

Triage

Yes, there are days when the ER doors explode
and Code Blue comes in on a gurney, rapid
crosstalk over the patients, one right after
the other. More often though,
we triage our lives with quiet, glancing
deferments of care, attention, faith, for whatever
needs us and cannot be ignored or left
to die. We have no choice but to choose
among these three — money, the people we love
and our inner life, such as it is. We can save
the one, maybe two out of three, but nobody
has it all. The math doesn't work that way,
though one might serve another, the church
of parenthood, perhaps, or creativity
that pays the bills. But marriages can fail
in the face of sudden money.
We can fall in love as our business
fades, or drive down avenues
of achievement, proud and blind.
We can die before we die.
We can hold our breath for years
and do, our dreams growing beautiful
as autumn leaves, golden and forgotten. Still,
we can find what feeds us in triage, an ascending
crisis of opportunities, thinking like nurses
and ER doctors, fast and wise
as much as possible, trying to live one life
as we save others.

Being of Two Minds

I'm less impressed with intelligence
than I used to be. A younger man,
I ached to have a mind
like a steel trap. Philosophy
was a kind of courage, practicing
how to be dead, how to live
without a body, and I loved
how it felt to think,
the calm regency of logic,
reading my way to heaven, detached
somehow and floating.
In truth, I was never that smart,
not like I wanted to be,
but who is? "Logic is such hell,"
said Whitehead to Russell, humoring
tons of *Principia Mathematica*
into place. I was watching a weightlifting
contest on cable the other night,
brothers taking on 500, 600 pounds
or more, everyone cheering but with alarm
as each man almost exploded.
Russell once proposed
a preemptive nuclear strike on Russia, thereby
preventing the next world war.
You can see the logic.

These days, a lake surrounded by forest
is on my mind, as my mind
is a kind of reservoir, green logic
with reason and growth supporting each other
like ivy loving the fences, gates, tree trunks,
anything it can wrap its arms around
to climb to the sun. Peering down,
let's say the water allows
a gradient understanding from light

to dark, like watching a bright bottle cap
sinking in the clear ocean, growing
smaller till the light of reason plays
out, and that is mystery, how
the mind can work by faith,
not keys unlocking locks designed
for keys, but a tender graduation
up and down, and maybe on the bottom,
interesting scum, low gardens of algae,
implements and iron contraptions
galore, turning to rust.
And let's not forget the cows
grazing overhead in Plato's heaven,
just standing there, the way they do, making
four holes in the grass, cow thoughts
furiously growing in the mind
like zucchini.

Riot Heart

Watching the riots at night, I see
myself on either side, in the eyes
of a terrified sheriff, clinched
and armored, fingers
tightening around the baton,
in the glorious looter
wrapped in wild flags of freedom,
the shuddering arc of a brick
through a plate-glass window, cars
overturned and set on fire, in the smoke
of truth and solid fictions outlawed
and re-enforced outside of law,
both sides joined in hot divisions
blinding a mortal, flashing republic.

A riot is years in the making, centuries
of obligations and mild neglect
crystallized into theft and helplessness.
So where is the revolution? How do I volunteer?
What can I sell in the shop of my heart
the morning after? Me with a broom,
sweeping up, restocking the shelves,
looking for more than a civil life
of blue skies and broken glass forever.

Burning the Books

Consider how beautifully the pages turn,
fluttering in the heat. They stiffen
and curl, black letters
melting into black.

People have died for these books,
been burned themselves, fingers
ripped from pages. History is over
and begins again with bright teachers
and a rushing spirit that unfolds its wings
and soars into great silence, embers
feeding on ashes like mystery.

Now is the time to unwrite the books, a conversion,
learning with all our heart and soul and mind and strength,
learning as if our lives were at stake, learning
in cold faith what we need
to burn.

Ashes

John Lacher, father-in-law, 1928-2010

Heavier than you'd think
if you think of ashes,
a man's worth
tucked in a box now
passed from one
relation to the next
as we scatter what remains
on Puget Sound, though
"scatter" is too light
a word. These ashes
plunge, I say
plunge into the cold,
clear water, bone chips
that even the straight
blast of the furnace couldn't finish.
If you had known this man,
even from a distance,
you would have felt
how hard he burned
himself with blind
and sturdy rage,
with diligent weight
he carried in love for others.
And if you had loved him,
even from a distance, you
weren't surprised how his dust
behaved like stars,
the million particles trailing
clouds of milky smoke
like galaxies, as beautiful
and constant as anything else
burning in the sky.

Gradual Empires

Determined as you are, remember
your strength is like water
slipping through the stubborn
clutch of mountain rocks, collapsing
into the polished faces to escape
boiling on the other side
and reform itself into easy streams
careering downward through clouds
of expanding canyons, defined
by the mountain as it moves
the mountain to the sea.

Remember this in the days of hard
stops and deadlines you work to create.
Remember as you scuffle and bleed,
as if you had no choice
but to shoulder the current,
fighting for rank and recognition
that only rises to the common
melt and overwhelming surrender
of a strength like water.

That Great Disparaging Choir in My Head

has work to do, it cannot stop, the steady bass notes
thrumming low, the rich and plummy voices
singing no, no way, you tender fraud,
grace notes of contempt
pitch perfect to my ear, and I should know.
I lead this choir, exorcise and conjure back
their murmuring, pre-emptive scorn just
sharp enough to feel like virtue.
We practice hard, making an art of bittersweet
discouragements with quiet, steady chants
of loser, loser, who do you think you are?
And naturally I'm both — my own dependent critic,
joined in stubborn harmony, doing the best we can.

Firing the Poem

Basically it's your attitude.
You sit by yourself, stewing
in a cubicle and sure,
you have your moments,
we all do, but some of us think
you're looking for a fight
and that's not how you build
a team, much less a business.
We're all here to make
a profit. Money talks
so what are you trying to say?
We want to treat you like a human being,
even though you're not, of course,
but you want art
that isn't. We respect that,
but you have to go.
Look, I'm on your side. I'm one
of the good guys, but show
me what you've got. Image is all.
That and R&D. And as for marketing,
when was the last time you
took a co-worker to lunch?
I'm not the greatest manager
in the world. I know that.
You know that. I just think —
and I'm not alone in this —
that we don't have a true fit here
between needs and resources.
It's odd. You're an in-and-outer,
sometimes brilliant, sometimes unprepared.
In some ways, you're better
than you think you are
but in some ways, not.
So look, it's getting dark.
Just sign this release

and you're free to go. Security
will walk you to the door.
I wish you the best,
and be careful out there. I mean that.
You were always a stranger.

Opportunities in Real Estate

I've reached that elevation
where what I learn climbing
higher will always be less
than what I've already forgotten.
My intellectual mortgage,
as it were, is underwater,
and yes, I still make payments,
but I may not make
good money on the deal.
To build, you need to forget
as much as remember.
My house is low and small.
Maybe years from now,
someone notices, someone buys,
a bookish family perhaps,
building memories with two
young kids and a bookish dog,
or an elderly, gay couple
knowing precisely
what to remodel. A fixer-
upper in other words,
a bargain in the long run
or at least until the neighborhood
settles back to what it was
some centuries ago, the wind
blowing over the graves
of old development.

A City Is the People You Know There

After too many years, I knock
and a stranger appears at the front door
of the creaky white Victorian. No, she doesn't live here
anymore and who are you?

All my friends have moved away
like me, taking their history with them,
but you and I could never change
what happened between us.
Then we do. Looking for a pleasant wound,
I go back to my private shelf and find
an empty space where my youth should be, with a note
in that still captivating hand of yours — *dear,*
thought you wouldn't mind.

Becoming Air

Slow pounding on the door
downstairs, a low, steady sound
more felt than heard, month
after month, for a year,
then almost two, now growing,
filling the massive house
where my sister waits
in her flying bed, exhausted,
with a painted battle scene above her head,
historic men on horseback, swords waving, charging
always toward victory.
Then a faint click.
Greatness enters the room,
pauses, as if questioning,
and offers a white flower. At last,
after years of framed achievement,
anger and controlling love,
she sighs, a burning fragment
cradled in the arms of pure death,
and together they descend with dignity,
intimate all the way down
the amazing stairs.

St. Francis in Prayer

I have no idea
what he thought as he felt
his way into darkness,
entering the massive
break in the granite mountain,
six feet wide at the mouth
and running for hundreds of yards
or more, who knows, growing
smaller, thinner, more
impossible
so a man like
Francis could touch
both walls with his arms
stretched out, then
with shoulders, then
with less. I can only imagine
how he could push
his small self
ever deeper each time,
past fear, past consolation, past
faith itself,
as if he could squeeze
into God inside of God, and there
he would pray, blind and silent, heart
slowing in the absolute dark.

That's how I see him,
and after hours, sometimes
days, he reemerges,
dragging his stupid body
up from the cave,
blinking in twilight,
and he stares for a time
at the inescapable beauty
of Umbria, and he prays

for nothing and the prayer
goes on, finding its way
through slips and fractures
where God creeps,
ever closer, ever more
impossibly
to the empty heart.

Song Without Words

I, too, can't stand it, the poem
adored and smothered
underneath a pillow of its own
dear wording, were it not
for the sometimes arrival
of poetry itself,
the spirit and soul,
the unspoken, inner life,
what used to be called a god,
erotic in all its majesty, a tenderness,
fluid and calmly joining
the same with the un-same,
loving like water and undenied,
an invisible oxygen by which we can see
new patterns, kinship, truth, call it
what you will.

So let us serve the song inside
the singing. Let us have poems
that cough, sputter
and soar like kites or plunge
to the ground, dragged
and helpless until they rise again
or not, poems like a lost
balloon ascending, hopeful, wobbly,
poems like a sneeze, like a pop
fly ball that arcs so beautifully into the sky
and disappears, spot poems
in a snarl of traffic, poems from the mother
folds of expression, ocean swells
of Ave Marias that rise —
a breath — and slowly fall
at the hour of our death, amen.
Poems like a proud flag stripped
naked and holy, sweet poems

like a vase of rare flowers
left on the kitchen table
for one who might never return,
poems like coded messages
aimed at the night sky with flashlights,
poems overwhelmed in wild surf
slammed against sea walls, spray shot
skyward with diamonds,
and poems like smoke,
like valleys open to the world,
doing their best work in silence, breathless,
living on language, running
out of words.

The Silence of God

Or maybe He never shuts up.
You tell me.

Think of supernovas and the blind
seed cracked open, ecstatic
with moisture, the utter generosity
of something
rather than nothing.

And here come the penguins.
Is that silence? In what language?

It's like this —
every morning God lifts
the nuclear sun in His bare hands
and remakes the world instant by instant
and not once does He say
"you owe me."

Darwin raised his doubts. Could a caterpillar
eaten alive from the inside out
by the larvae of a parasitic
wasp be the art of God's love? The very idea...
And yes, the God of hurricanes
and stillborns, our Lord of disease
and life-giving death.

I recognize His touch, His wicked
humor and His tenderness,
all of us
His masterpieces,
no choice and no exceptions.

So I ask God, "Am I making You up?"
And He speaks to me. "Honey,
of course you are."

The true, the original work
comes out of the blue
and God is the blue.

Opening Windows

I pick at the window locks painted over with layers of enamel. An archeology of decisions and fashions. Designer white, then blue underneath, then a Fifties kind of mustard yellow. I hammer at the frame. I tease and cajole. I seduce. The air in the room is becoming hot and thick. I've learned all I can, and I'm tired of living like this. I throw my shoulder against the window, hard. Nothing. Then again. Nothing. Have faith! Use your head! I butt against the frame and finally it opens with a sharp crack, like an old joint, a reluctant admission. I push harder and the window opens wide and fresh air pours into the room, sea air with the smell of salt, and I breathe deeply, closing my eyes.

I move from window to window, the stubborn room growing lively, curtains billowing, papers trembling on my desk, then flying off, whirlwinds of paper, most of a lifetime's work. On the shelves, the slim books shiver and decline. I watch their beautifully carved letters disappearing into the page like invisible ink, moist but unreadable. My brilliant career.

So what, I tell myself. We still have choices. I take off my clothes. In front of me, the ocean spreads to the horizon, cold tons of water, silent and intense, somehow seething with promise. Ragged storm clouds come walking over the hills. Then a tornado appears in the distance and a barn explodes, the logical framework flying apart in the roar of a vacuum, jagged lumber knifing and tumbling through the air. On one side the ocean, on the other the storm, like a painting that's alive in a wonderful, terrible way.

Understanding Markets

Like God, invisible but apparent everywhere, like whispers and rumors of exchange in a private language of default swaps and synthetic obligations, like money touching itself, like a weather of expectations, buffeted by incarnations of credit, roving mysteries entertained by algorithms and heavy machinery, data flashing with treasure, like a song, like blood, like a trillion drops of water so tiny they float by themselves, careless and random until they cool, lose interest and collapse. Like clouds, mere clouds, and clouds weigh tons. Let's not forget that.

leaning against the ATM
eyes closed
as if in prayer

Deepwater Horizon

As if by torchlight, I remember the years
I went down to the energy
capital of the world to write for clients
in oil and gas, to follow great engines of commerce,
tax regimes and the audits floating on oceans of credit.
I remember the semi-retired world leaders
showing up in the lobbies, flanked by vigilance,
billionaires on the jumbotrons.
It was that kind of world, impressive, strange,
dead serious but somehow made up
and embraced because
it worked. I would file my stories
of who said what and where we're going,
and in the evening I would walk to dinner
past luxury gallerias, looking up
at the office towers. They seemed to float like mountains
filled with light, so clean, empty and quiet.

On the third day we reemerged, blinking in sunlight,
sharing cabs to the airport, but I would linger
for an afternoon to look at art nearby,
treasures in a museum built with oil,
the million-dollar abstractions, sepulchers,
one lonely masterpiece and always
the dim chapel next door where I would sit
in peace with the huge, transcendent paintings, so dark
and yet with an unexpected hope, as if
at the end of the world.

That was my job, to explain how some things
work and what they cost, so let me remember
the long drive home at night, thinking,
as we might do when we drive through the dark,
how all our computers run on fire,
terminals linked to the server farms burning

with algorithms cooled by the rain,
smartphones embedded
with beads of blood, the networks
alive in a cloud of lightning
charged by the power of crude,
and let me remember,
as if by torchlight, the offshore rig,
the flash and explosion, steel
groaning as the burning platform
drops to its knees, mercy boats
circling, helpless, and the columns of fire
ascending in darkness, images
Shakespearean in grandeur, bodies
of angels floating in water.

Best Practices

Admission

Perhaps in heaven, the blind
will still be blind, the lame
won't walk, the deformed will not
be otherwise, and it won't
make a difference. Not a bit. Perhaps
all of heaven is just two
inches away, the earth made
truly in the image of heaven. Hard
to say. If it's heaven all the way to heaven,
then it might be hell all the way to hell. We see
glimpses in the eyes of the patient dead
walking among us. So too,
in a heaven filled with children
already here. Somehow, this is it. We have all arrived,
a dazzling, infinite world packed
neatly inside our capacities.
If only we could see with both eyes open
what we see with both eyes closed, and perhaps
we always have.

Outsider Art

For the blind seer Hawkins Bolden, Archie Byron dignified, for Ralph Griffin and his stalking roots, then Bessie Harvey (with little caps on each right doll), for the prophet Lonnie Holley, James Hampton beside his Throne, for Charlie Lucas the Tin Man, Herbert Singleton Jr., storyteller, Mary T. Smith filling up her yard, for Bill Traylor and his twiggy figures, stoneman William Edmondson, dear Georgia Speller, Henry Speller, Moze Tolliver who signs his name, for carver Jesse Aaron, Jimmie Lee Sudduth's hands for brushes, Purvis Young in blue-eyed prison, Thorton Dial and family everywhere and all the diligent unknown others

God is the unexpected.
God is junk.

So out of junk and abandon, out of busted
nickel and the power of God, out of cast-offs and defects
picked over, spent with ample grime
I make this charm
out-rigged and harmonized,
embedded in rank and sour development,
hanging thread-
like, unfolding out of three boxes in the mind
with roots dangling,
out of magic markers, TV plastic,
pink costume jewelry, rusted bedsprings, rivets and twine,
full-throated with the human head
of a tea kettle upside down
with the spout for a nose and two eyes
punched in on either side, the third
on top to see God coming,
crowned with thorny fences
spiked against fat demons quick to bite
and Satan (subtle breather) on his spider toes.

Be calm. Be born. You're healed. You're saved.
So Jesus crushes death between His teeth.
So art comes back as teaching art, blind eggs for eyes

and double-sighted, stubborn roots
hauled up and dripping holy colors,
art that escapes
outside and deep within, deformed
so it can breathe, an art overlooked
and rescued so the mind can see on fire.

So we ask the prophet Lonnie, What are you doing on that mountaintop?
and Lonnie says I'm trying
to undo hell.

Learning to Paint

I worked with the older painters,
union men and slow as Christmas,
but their style was perfection,
laying down a thick coat of enamel
over intricate moldings, frames and trim
with long, seamless strokes. No brush marks, no drips.
They never used tape, not even for windows.
"Better a good brush and a steady hand."
They taught me attention and care,
cleaning and double cleaning the bristles
in solvent, then water and soap, then wash again.
All winter we detailed a white mansion
overlooking a snow-covered lake.
The owner was head of HR for Giant Seeds,
a family man, and he spent the season with his wife
in a lavish Florida splashed with green.
The house was empty, just me and the three men
in white, painting white, disappearing into our work
on schedule, and we finished the day before
he returned, gathering our brushes and drop cloths,
leaving nothing behind, spotless, calm, as if
we were never there.

Rothko's Chapel

At first you see nothing,
eyes adapting to the low light,
sky light from above,
and then, out of the dark
plum, deep russet
and oxblood so nearly black
it's more than black,
emerges a slow radiance,
a generosity
of auras becoming thresholds,
maps and open windows
opening the night,
art nailed
to fourteen panels,
each station one less
terminal, each terminal
our next beginning.

Staring at God, these paintings,
if that's what they really are,
become incarnate, beyond our insight,
faith, definition and all
the powers of illumination,
and we see the truth. This dark
and ascending sacrifice, this light, this mortal
beauty will save the world.

Home Depot

I love the smell of lumber late at night,
the possibilities of smooth, clean planks
and finely sanded boards. No ideas but in things
tonight and the things are beautiful — the sharp,
ready teeth of power saws, bright hammers and precision drills.
Lethal in their own way. Inspiring.

Outside in the parking lot, a soft, steady wind
from the dark Gulf. The stronger we become, the more
we're afraid. In the great, unraveling journey westward,
we took what was open and made it empty, though that emptiness
is beautiful as well. We work so hard in this country,
as if we had nothing to lose. In subdivisions,
lights are turning off in the dream homes, one by one.
An almost nation, atomic and still. Homebuilders,
we do it ourselves.

Walking in Circles

I get lost easily, even now,
entering the dim, allegorical woods
preserved inside our city, always
the faint, white noise of traffic
somewhere beyond the trees as I wander
with diligence down a dirt path beaten
by others and myself. I'm on my way
I think, until I think I've been this way
before not twenty minutes ago. I'm never sure.
Nothing is a straight line
or even a labyrinth but a squirrelly maze
I trace and retrace almost every day
for whatever thoughts that might arrive
as I walk in circles, truer circles described
inside of circles, having learned
I need to get lost, a parade of one,
to find my calling, then lost again
to find my own way home.

Learning Mountain

Old man deliberately takes
his time on the steep, irregular

dragon vein of stairs
ascending to a mountain shrine

fixed in the clouds. He pauses
to catch his breath, then grips

the handrail and pulls
himself to the next stone step.

The sun feels pleasant on his back.
Children with their little wings

float past him. A little smile,
watching them play. This high up,

he can barely hear the traffic below,
cars and light trucks, the snarl

and flow of impatience.
He climbs past old graves,

watching for tigers, his thoughts
dragging and bumping along behind him.

By late afternoon, he arrives.
What progress! He opens

the screen door and steps inside.
The shrine is deserted.

Each wall is filled with antique demons,
parched and faded in the wind.

Birds have nested in the rafters,
and in front of him, three

unexpected angels
and the Lord of Peace.

He eats his little sandwich
outside on the porch, eyes closed.

All around him, the mountains are breathing.
Great rivers in the sky…

When he wakes up, the light is falling.
He's stayed too long.

When will he learn? And what?
He could sleep all night on this mountain,

freezing at an altitude where life
hardens, becoming deathlike and brittle,

and what would be the use
of that, he thinks. Hot tea, he thinks.

Truth is alive and the truth
finds us. Far below, a white crane

rides the slow clouds of the valley.
Dizzy, he steadies himself.

Strong bones, he thinks
and lets himself ease

downward to the mother
darkness on the other side.

Manifest Destiny

Raise the white flags beautifully,
great flags of shocking silk unfolding,
billowing above our homes
and the homes of all our neighbors,
flags over quiet, hurting towns
and stubborn factories,
our last, heroic cities winding down
from open fields to vacant lots,
a thousand flags released into darkness,
signals in the wind across our vast,
lonely and anxious nation.

History whispers in our ear — *If you even*
think about fighting, you've already lost.
If you win, you lose. If you lose
you lose. So this is my dream — an army
of white flags lifted in overwhelming surrender.
No borders, no walls, no demarcations
scratched in crumbling concrete. This is my dream —
we have won the peace, an enduring republic,
infinitely yielding, falling and rising
again with the wind.

ICU, Four a.m.

In the dark, everyone is kind.
Nurse Ho gently taps along my arm,
looking for a possible vein. People
from all over the world are rushing
to help me. The hospitalist from India
asks, "Do you know where you are?
Who's the president? What month is it?"
These seem like important questions
but somehow difficult. Impossible.
"Make a fist," she says, inserting the slow drip.
My compass needle wobbles, confused.
Do I know where I am?
Some sort of mid-point. Or not. I loosen my grip.
Strong hands carry me through the dark.
The journey has already started.

After the Accident

Only after my wife appears at the door
and tells me our younger son
can't talk, has been in an accident, something
about a collision, and we rush out,
speeding to the intersection, backed-up traffic, and I park
sideways off the shoulder, we're running now,
out of breath, and we enter the clearing of police, an ambulance,
glass shattered everywhere, and our son's car,
front end smashed, filled with air bags,
and a van with a mom and two little kids
who seem okay, she's talking to officers, and suddenly
there he is, shaking violently, and I hold him,
and he's crying in my arms, saying, "I'm so sorry, so sorry,"
and I'm telling him it doesn't matter, he's not hurt,
nobody's hurt, and he turns to his mom, and I stand there,
not knowing what else to do, and only weeks later,
after he and I drove out to the wrecking yard,
one last check to clean out the glove box, looking for keys,
only then do I try to say something dadlike and wise, a mystery
about the size of a football, something I could pass along
as we followed the watchman in his little golf cart
through rows of unlucky cars. I say that perhaps
the best we can do is to better name the accident we never
quite see coming. I quote the boxer, "Everybody's got a plan
till they get punched." I say the cars remind me
of a drive-in theater, and we're all just watching
the movie of the present day. "What do you think?" I ask.
And he, my son the unexpected, the one I think will go
much further than I will toward some unknown destination,
tells me, "No, these cars are more like snapshots."
"Of what?" I ask. "Of fear," he says.

How Much Does Your House Weigh?

Somewhere in the middle of marriage,
we did the math. Two hundred pounds
per square foot times twenty nine hundred
square feet. That's five hundred eighty
thousand pounds, three hundred tons almost
we carried on wings. For twenty years
the rooms were filled with children, noisy, unmindful
about the future, as was their right. We gave them
memories, and you filled the backyard with roses,
antiques from abandoned cemeteries, bred
to survive alone, Heaven on Earth, Rêve d'Or,
Belinda's Dream, and a marriage bed
of Icebergs, white and burgundy.
We raised the boys in the middle
class of expectations. I taught them to fly,
wobbly on their bicycles, how to drive, how to leave
home someday while you would show them
how to stay in love. This was our calling,
the art of effacement except for the home
you made and the house I strained to support,
and under it all a thin, insinuation of debt
corrupting our slab foundation.
"This debt is a cancer," you said,
and you were right. I made a mistake
when I married you, and your mistake
was to marry me. We did the math,
and we're both bad at numbers.
But what counts more — planting a tree
or writing a poem? Writing a book
or raising a child? Somehow the boys grew up
and away, now fine young men, and now we carry
half the weight with a smaller house, though
even that might be too much. Tonight,
I see us in a Liberty Belle, a bomber
from World War II, coming back from a night raid.

I'm not a pilot but I'm flying this thing,
your hand on mine as my hand rests on the throttle.
We've taken hits, the plane bucks and shivers,
air whistling through the cabin, smoke
trailing from one of the engines,
almost out of fuel, on a glide path
downward across the divided Channel,
your hand on mine, the both of us still working,
pressing to reach some green,
imaginary and ultimate England.

About the Author

Richard Cole is the author of two books of poetry: *The Glass Children* (The University of Georgia Press) and *Success Stories* (Limestone Books). He is also the author of a memoir, *Catholic by Choice* (Loyola Press). His poems and essays have appeared in numerous publications and anthologies. Honors include an NEA fellowship and several writing grants. In addition, Cole has worked as a copywriter in New York, served as a communications manager in four software startups, edited two trade journals, and now runs a business writing agency in Austin, Texas. More at richard-cole.net.

CPSIA information can be obtained
at www.ICGtesting.com
Printed in the USA
LVHW020716031221
704917LV00003B/61